The Gi Daughter and the Hunting Dog

written by Peter Wallace
illustrated by Constance Bergum

McGraw-Hill School Division
New York Farmington

Storyteller: This happened. There were two villages. One was high on the mesa, the other low in the valley near the river. Every day the men went out hunting for food. The men from the high mesa village caught rabbits and deer. In the river village, the men came back with nothing. The Chief did not know how to help his village. The daughter of the Chief came to speak to her father.

Chief's Daughter: Father, I walked up to the other village. I waited and watched. I saw that they have a cat. The cat helps them hunt. I must find something to help us.

Storyteller: That night, Old Spider Woman sent a dream to the girl.

Old Spider Woman: There is an animal that can help you hunt. It is smaller than a deer and larger than a rabbit. It can keep you company, and smell out food or danger.

Storyteller: Next morning, the girl told her father her dream.

Chief: I have heard of this animal. It is called a dog. To find one, you will have to take a trip to the village of the Great Dogs. This village is very far away, so you must be careful on your trip.

Storyteller: The people of the river village prepared food for Chief's Daughter to take on her journey. Soon she was on her way.

Storyteller: On the third day of her trip, in a dark forest, the girl saw Old Spider Woman. Next to her was a very large snake.

Old Spider Woman: Ah, here you are! Don't let him scare you. It was I who put the dream in your head. I will change myself into a tiny spider and go with you to show you the way.

Chief's Daughter: Thank you, Grandmother Spider.

Storyteller: Old Spider Woman made herself small and sat on Chief's Daughter's shoulder.

Old Spider Woman: The snake will take us where we need to go. Hop on!

Storyteller: The girl sat behind the snake's head. Off they flew to the north, the wind whistling loudly.

Chief's Daughter: Grandmother Spider, how much farther?

Old Spider Woman: The dog village is on the top of this mountain.

Storyteller: As they neared the top, the girl heard a harsh barking sound.

Chief's Daughter: What is that?

Old Spider Woman: That is the bark of a dog.

Storyteller: Just then, a dog ran towards a pond. Chief's Daughter watched in surprise as the dog went down a ladder into the pond and disappeared under the water.

Old Spider Woman: Go now, Daughter of the Chief!

Storyteller: The girl ran to the pond. The water parted as she climbed down the ladder. Then the pond closed like a door above her head. She was in the village of the Great Dogs.

Auntie Dog: Well! A person. What do you want?

Storyteller: Old Spider Woman whispered into the girl's ear.

Old Spider Woman: Be very sweet to Auntie! Don't make her mad.

Chief's Daughter: I have come to find a dog to help my village with our hunting. The village on the high mesa has a cat. They catch rabbits and deer. Our hunters catch nothing.

Auntie Dog: Why not search for a cat?

Chief's Daughter: Because Grandmother Spider sent me a dream. It told me that dogs can smell out food or danger and keep people company.

Auntie Dog: She is right. But tell me, why should I let you have one?

Chief's Daughter: Because you are good and kind, Auntie Dog. Here. These are presents from my people.

Storyteller: The girl gave Auntie Dog the basket of food from the village. This time when Auntie Dog spoke, her voice was kind.

Auntie Dog: Ah! You have a dear heart. You may take one dog.

Storyteller: She whistled to the whole village. Dogs in all shapes, sizes, and colors rushed to Auntie Dog's side.

Auntie Dog: Play the music!

Storyteller: And they danced for Chief's Daughter.

Chief's Daughter: I will choose that large black one with the spot.

Auntie Dog: Ah! You have made a good choice. This is the best hunter of them all. Now. You must always be kind to your dog. Treat your dog well, and you will have good luck. Promise?

Chief's Daughter: I promise.

Storyteller: So, gliding on the snake's back with Old Spider Woman on her shoulder, the girl returned to her village. Her family was very happy to see her and to meet the dog.

Chief: So this is what a dog looks like.

Storyteller: They washed and brushed its fur. They gave it cold water to drink and food to eat. In time, it became a great hunter. Rabbits and deer and good luck came to the village.